CHARACTER

MARIA CELIA, 36, the older sister

SOFIA, 24, the younger sister

LIEUTENANT PORTUONDO, a man in his 30s

MILITIA GUARD, a man in his 30s played by the actor playing
   Victor Manuel

VICTOR MANUEL, a man in his 30s

PLACE

Cuba. A spacious colonial house.

TIME

1991.

Note to designers: The set and lights should have a feeling of openness. They should not feel claustrophobic.

TWO SISTERS AND A PIANO

Prologue

THE SEARCH

A Victorian sofa and side table are stage left. A baby grand piano is downstage right. Music plays, then in full darkness we hear the loud sound of a metal prison door closing. Shadowy lights slowly come up to reveal two militia guards in green uniforms at the Obispo house doing a search. The electricity has been cut off. The guards hold flashlights, which they aim at different parts of the room. The sound of furniture turning over, glass breaking, objects falling on the floor. Militia Guard pushes Sofia and goes after Maria Celia.

MILITIA GUARD.   LIEUTENANT PORTUONDO.
Tell us where you hide them.   Come on, tell us.
Tell us where you keep them.   Come on …
MARIA CELIA. I don't know what you're talking about!
SOFIA. She's not hiding anything!
MILITIA GUARD. Liar … You're lying. We want all the papers you're hiding.
SOFIA. She's not hiding any papers.
LIEUTENANT PORTUONDO. Just tell us where you keep them, bitch! Go get your writing.
SOFIA. Don't hurt her or I'll hit you with this chair.
LIEUTENANT PORTUONDO. Just tell us where you hide them.
MARIA CELIA. Hide what! Hide what!

| SOFIA. | MARIA CELIA. |
| She's got nothing! | I don't have anything. |

SOFIA.
She's got nothing!
She's got nothing!
She's not hiding anything!

MILITIA GUARD. You shut up bitch!

MARIA CELIA. I already told you ...

SOFIA. She already told you ...

MILITIA GUARD. You shut up, you big mouth or I'll cut off your tongue! I'll cut off your tongue! — Where do you keep your writing?

MARIA CELIA. I've got nothing! ... I've got nothing hidden, compañero!

LIEUTENANT PORTUONDO. Let's start the inventory, Mena.

MILITIA GUARD. Who does inspection here every week?

MARIA CELIA. Polita ... Polita Mirabal.

MILITIA GUARD. (To Lieutenant Portuondo.) Polita Mirabal ... Polita Mirabal.

LIEUTENANT PORTUONDO. The girls have had enough.

MILITIA GUARD. Yeah they've had enough. A bunch of weaklings. We got two lesbos in here. A writer and a pianist. Which one is the pianist? (Sofia raises her hand.) Play something on the piano. I have a headache. (Gives Lieutenant Portuondo a file.) See if you can figure out these papers. It's a bunch of rice and mangoes. (Walks around, inspects the place with his flashlight.) This is a big house for just two people. Who else you've got living here — ghosts?

LIEUTENANT PORTUONDO. I can't figure out this shit either.

MILITIA GUARD. We'll leave it blank. What's the pianist doing? I told you to play something. (Sofia goes to the piano.) Let's start the inventory. A piano.

LIEUTENANT PORTUONDO. Piano check.

MILITIA GUARD. A sofa.

LIEUTENANT PORTUONDO. Sofa check.

MILITIA GUARD. A small oak table.

LIEUTENANT PORTUONDO. Oak table check.

MILITIA GUARD. A radio.

LIEUTENANT PORTUONDO. Radio check. (Sofia plays the piano.)

MILITIA GUARD. Brass lamp.

LIEUTENANT PORTUONDO. Brass lamp check. (Lights slowly come up on Maria Celia standing on the rooftop.)

MILITIA GUARD. Rocking chair.

LIEUTENANT PORTUONDO. Rocking chair check.

MILITIA GUARD. Picture of a lady with a fan.

LIEUTENANT PORTUONDO. Picture check. *(Lights start to fade on the guards. Maria Celia is in full light now holding a letter, which she folds and places in her pocket as she speaks to her husband in the distance.)*

MARIA CELIA. "Antonio, my dear husband: I'm standing on top of this roof, wanting to leap into the sky and send you this letter. Almost three months and two weeks now and not a word from you. Today a few militia guards came to search the house. They took inventory of all our things. I don't know what this means. This is usually done when somebody is leaving the country. Yesterday we heard on the radio about amnesty for political prisoners, so I'm keeping my fingers crossed. I tell Sofie that 1991 is our lucky year. We've been allowed back home. At least here we can walk all the way from the kitchen to the living room, and that's a long distance compared to the size of our cell back in prison. It seems that there are so many things happening out there in the world, my love … A new way of thinking … Freedom … I always tell Sofie how much I love the leader Gorbachev, any man who has a birthmark that looks like an island on his forehead is a blessed man. I'm writing a new story, my love, which I'm sending you a page at a time. It's what keeps me going. The writing. The man and the woman in my new story. They take me out of this house. Their walks to the sea. I miss you more and more, my love. A big kiss and a hug, Maria Celia." *(Allegro piano music is heard. Lights slowly come up on Sofia playing the piano, as lights fade down on Maria Celia. She climbs down from the roof.)*

9

ACT ONE

Scene 1

THE MAN BEHIND THE WALL
AND THE LOST LETTERS

Sofia is playing the piano. Maria Celia walks toward her. Suddenly, Sofia stops playing.

MARIA CELIA. Why did you stop?

SOFIA. Shshhh …

MARIA CELIA. But you were playing so beautifully …

SOFIA. *(Whispering.)* I thought I heard something.

MARIA CELIA. What?

SOFIA. *(Whispers.)* Next door. *(They both speak in low voices.)*

MARIA CELIA. I didn't hear anything. You think he's home? That's probably your imagination. Play that song again. *(Sofia presses her ear to the wall.)*

SOFIA. *(Whispering.)* No … Listen. Come close to the wall. *(Maria Celia moves close to the wall.)*

MARIA CELIA. *I don't hear a thing.*

SOFIA. Shshhhh … I did. You hear that?

MARIA CELIA. *(Walks away from the wall.)* Nonsense. That's the wind or a cat walking on top of the roof. There's nobody there.

SOFIA. Yesterday he came around this time. I heard him.

MARIA CELIA. Where was I?

SOFIA. Where else? You were up on the roof writing.

He sat by the doorway with a drink in his hand. He smoked and drank and listened to me for more than an hour.

Music is like medicine. I touched his soul.

MARIA CELIA. Bah. You're falling in love with an invisible man.

SOFIA. You can still love a person and not be physical.

MARIA CELIA. Then it turns into a lie. A lie of the heart. That's for young girls who fall in love with a man in a book or a movie.

You're twenty-four years old, and you know very well that people like him don't like people like us.

SOFIA. You like to press your ear to the wall as much as I do.

MARIA CELIA. I listen when I'm bored and tired and fed up with this house. Don't roll your eyes at me. You stand next to this wall every five minutes. I don't know what could be so interesting about him.

SOFIA. I heard him tell his friend how much he wanted to lie in bed with the two of us.

MARIA CELIA. Yep … A rotten, putrid mind he has!

SOFIA. He must see something in us, Maria Celia.

MARIA CELIA. Yes I can see what he sees. Two women unable to go out the door, under house arrest. A harem next to his house — Wake up, Sofia! Can't you see he's a dog! You've heard what he does when he's on duty. He sneaks a woman into the marina. He makes love to her all over his paperwork. Can't you see what kind of man he is — what goes through his head?

SOFIA. I still think it would be an adventure. You on this side of the bed, and me on this other side. We'll drive him wild and crazy, to the point that he'll go to work hypnotized in a trance. Then he'll drop dead from all the rapture, and there on his tomb will be inscribed: "Here I rest in peace for loving the Obispo sisters."

MARIA CELIA. I'm starting to think you have canaries inside your head. Let's go back to work. You're too naive, sometimes. The other night I had a dream with Mami. I swear she looked as if she had come down from the sky. I saw her standing at the end of a road, and I could hear her voice, "Celita, my child … Sofie, my hummingbird … Don't let the dirty communists brainwash you … Don't forget to place a glass of water on the altar for the angels. They get thirsty from watching over you. Teach your sister to walk through life. Pin a prayer to the hem of her dress."

SOFIA. Did she say that? *(Smiles.)* Poor Mami …

MARIA CELIA. *(Produces a small piece of paper from inside the piano.)* I wrote something on a piece of paper. I was going to pin it to your dress without telling you, but then I thought of putting it inside the piano.

SOFIA. What is it?

MARIA CELIA. A prayer. Let me have the hem of your dress. *(Kneels down to pin it to Sofia's dress. There is a knock at the door. Maria Celia goes to the entranceway and listens. Sofia stays at a distance.)*

SOFIA. *(Whispering.)* Who is it?

MARIA CELIA. Shssh … I don't know … *(Listens for a moment, then loudly.)* Who is it?

LIEUTENANT PORTUONDO. Lieutenant Portuondo, open up. *(Maria Celia throws up her arms, expressing to her sister the burden of the visit. She opens the door. Lieutenant Portuondo comes in.)*

MARIA CELIA. If you're here for inspection, we had inspection two days ago.

LIEUTENANT PORTUONDO. *(Enters the space as if he owned it.)* No. I'm not here for inspection. I came to talk to you.

MARIA CELIA. What can I do for you, Lieutenant?

LIEUTENANT PORTUONDO. It looks as if you're not well disposed towards visitors, compañera.

MARIA CELIA. What can I do for you?

LIEUTENANT PORTUONDO. This letter …

MARIA CELIA. I wrote it.

LIEUTENANT PORTUONDO. Well I received it a few days ago …

MARIA CELIA. I sent it to the ministry.

LIEUTENANT PORTUONDO. Then we need to talk. We need to have a private conversation. *(Looks at Sofia. She exits. He strolls around the room.)* Your letter is more like a petition or an application. What sort of thing are you applying for?

MARIA CELIA. I'm asking you to put an end to the postal theft. You hold up all my letters from abroad. You open up all my correspondence, I haven't received a letter from my husband in over three months.

LIEUTENANT PORTUONDO. *(Smiles.)* You're absolutely beautiful, compañera. I remember the first day they brought you to the ministry. I couldn't look at you too much. *(Opens file.)* I must say this picture on your file doesn't do you justice. I should try to get a photographer in here and photograph you again.

MARIA CELIA. I don't like to have my picture taken, Lieutenant. Can you do something about my mail, or not?

LIEUTENANT PORTUONDO. I suppose I can do a lot about your mail. *(Opens his knapsack. Pulls out two packs of letters tied up with a black ribbon.)* You receive a considerable amount of correspondence. Dangerous correspondence. Someone found a weapon inside a letter the other day. I was informed that one of our officers at the post office almost bled to death. They found these razor blades inside an envelope. *(Produces razor blades.)*

MARIA CELIA. They shouldn't have gone through my mail.

LIEUTENANT PORTUONDO. Is that a provocation, compañera?

MARIA CELIA. I just want …

LIEUTENANT PORTUONDO. Is somebody sending you razor blades so you can slice someone's throat? Or are you going to do some harm to yourself?

MARIA CELIA. Those are for my legs, Lieutenant. To shave my legs.

LIEUTENANT PORTUONDO. Our Soviet razors don't cut it for you.

MARIA CELIA. I thought we were going to talk about my mail.

LIEUTENANT PORTUONDO. We are talking about your mail. The razors. *(Sofia enters.)*

SOFIA. *(Interrupting.)* Would you like some water, Lieutenant?

LIEUTENANT PORTUONDO. No, thank you, compañera.

SOFIA. Maria Celia?

MARIA CELIA. No, thank you. *(Sofia exits.)*

LIEUTENANT PORTUONDO. This sort of thing is considered a weapon, illegal … Don't you know that?

MARIA CELIA. I didn't send it, Lieutenant.

LIEUTENANT PORTUONDO. *(Pulls out a small sample package of moisturizing lotion.)* I gather this is for your legs, too … Lotion de rose … Smells of roses, France. Who is this Monsieur Lamont? He writes to you often, sends you lots of things. Did you give your legs to this man?

MARIA CELIA. Look you don't have the right …

LIEUTENANT PORTUONDO. Are you in love with this man?

MARIA CELIA. I don't think that's important …

LIEUTENANT PORTUONDO. Was he your lover?

MARIA CELIA. No.

LIEUTENANT PORTUONDO. No?

MARIA CELIA. He's a friend.

LIEUTENANT PORTUONDO. And all the romantic letters.

MARIA CELIA. I don't know about any romantic letters.

LIEUTENANT PORTUONDO. You don't know about any romantic letters?

MARIA CELIA. No, I don't know. How would I know when I don't get any mail?

LIEUTENANT PORTUONDO. You're pretty good at keeping a straight face when you lie. Your husband in America is slipping correspondence through France, using the name André Lamont. I have them all here.

MARIA CELIA. I don't know what you're talking about.

LIEUTENANT PORTUONDO. You know exactly what I am talking about!

MARIA CELIA. *(With contained anger.)* Why do you keep on insisting that I know, that I know?! What am I supposed to know?! What am I supposed to do when I live in this hole! *(Pause. Takes hold of herself.)* Please — I am not asking for much.

LIEUTENANT PORTUONDO. I can't give you any mail — not when your husband is going to every Human Rights Commission, spreading bile against our system. Not when he's trying to publish your book in France. You must know all about it. I have all the information here: "Les Editions de Minuit will publish in October the translation of *The Seagrape*, by Maria Celia Obispo." *(Mockingly.)* Imagine compañera ... Foi, foi ... La vie shoo, shoo ... Just a few months from now your book will be all over France, Europe. Isn't that something, compañera?

Makes me hungry, that name — Minuit. Reminds me of mignon, filet mignon. It's amazing that a word like that can make your mouth water. Means midnight in French, doesn't it?

A lot of money, this Minuit company — Your father and your husband are going to get rich from your books. Lots of lonely people out there in the world — empty beds ... I've been reading one of your books. That's my new bed companion. Can you believe it, compañera?

MARIA CELIA. People should read whatever they like.

LIEUTENANT PORTUONDO. What makes you think I like your books?

MARIA CELIA. Who cares what I think, Lieutenant? You could be one of those people who reads books to fall asleep at night.

LIEUTENANT PORTUONDO. Oh, I read for meaning, compañera ... What was that line I like so much in your story? "There was that fugitive night in her." — Is that the way it goes?

You don't know what those words do to me. Does that surprise you, compañera, that I'm reading your book?

MARIA CELIA. Nothing surprises me, Lieutenant.

LIEUTENANT PORTUONDO. Well, I don't see the big fuss about your books. All the delegations say they're bourgeois propaganda, antirevolutionary, people's blood boils with indignation, but I'm not of the same opinion. I'm probably your number-one fan.

MARIA CELIA. Oh, just give it up, Lieutenant! I've gone through all the mind games! *(Sofia comes in with a coffee tray.)*

SOFIA. Café. I made some café ... Thought you would like some, Lieutenant.

LIEUTENANT PORTUONDO. Why don't you tell your sister that I didn't come here to do her harm.

SOFIA. I hope not. *(He takes a cup.)* If you kill her, she'll come back from the dead, right Maria Celia? *(Smiles. Takes sides with her.)* She'll pull you away by the feet when you're asleep and haunt you for the rest of your life. You don't know my sister.

LIEUTENANT PORTUONDO. Yes, you're right, I don't know your sister. *(Sipping coffee and looking at her.)* But I'd sure like to get to know her.

SOFIA. Maria Celia … The lieutenant is talking about you. He wants to get to know you. You want café?

MARIA CELIA. No.

SOFIA. Is that the mail you have in your knapsack? If you give her the mail you'll be on her good side.

LIEUTENANT PORTUONDO. And what's her good side like?

SOFIA. He wants to know about your good side, Maria Celia.

MARIA CELIA. Did you start cooking the beans?

SOFIA. They're cooking. They're cooking all right. *(Looks at him, then at her.)* There's a good side to her cooking, I can tell you that much.

LIEUTENANT PORTUONDO. So she's a good cook.

SOFIA. The best chicken fricassee in town.

LIEUTENANT PORTUONDO. Best chicken fricassee.

SOFIA. Get her a chicken. Give her the mail, and she'll make you chicken fricassee.

LIEUTENANT PORTUONDO. Is it true that you're a good cook?

MARIA CELIA. Am I going to get anything out of this?! Am I going to get my mail or do I have to put myself through a hunger strike?! Do I have to starve to get somebody's attention?! …

LIEUTENANT PORTUONDO. I'm sorry, compañera. I can't let you read about your husband's tactics.

MARIA CELIA. I don't care about his tactics. I just want to know about him. If he's dead or alive, if he's sick or in good health! If he's still my husband for God's sake!

LIEUTENANT PORTUONDO. If he's still your husband! … So he is your husband!

MARIA CELIA. Please … compañero, if you don't mind, I'd like you to go now.

LIEUTENANT PORTUONDO. No, I'm not leaving till we finish this talk. Let me give you some advice, compañera … You should write a letter to your husband and let him know that all those public denunciations he made, maybe got you out of prison, but that's not going to get you out of this country ... Do you understand? This concerns you too, Sofia. *(To Maria Celia.)* If you want to write him about this, I'll make sure your letter gets to him.

MARIA CELIA. Thank you, Lieutenant.

LIEUTENANT PORTUONDO. *(Strolls around the room.)* When do you usually write your stories, compañera? *(Silence. Sofia looks at Maria Celia and makes her way to her.)*

SOFIA. She doesn't write, Lieutenant. She stopped writing.

LIEUTENANT PORTUONDO. Oh, I know she writes. Her husband talks about a story she was going to send him. A new story. Something about a man and a woman in a glass tower, stolen boats ... I want to know if I could read it.

MARIA CELIA. I never finished it. I threw it away.

LIEUTENANT PORTUONDO. Is it a love story? *(Pause.)* I'm asking you if it's a love story!

SOFIA. Her stories are always about love, Lieutenant.

LIEUTENANT PORTUONDO. Can I have a moment alone with your sister?

SOFIA. Sure. *(Exits.)*

LIEUTENANT PORTUONDO. So what happened to this story?

MARIA CELIA. I threw it away.

LIEUTENANT PORTUONDO. What if I pay you to write it again?

MARIA CELIA. That would be a risk, don't you think? Or have you forgotten why we're still locked up in here?

LIEUTENANT PORTUONDO. It seems like everything is — my asking you to accept payment — my standing here talking to you about this ...

MARIA CELIA. It's not the same. You are the lieutenant.

LIEUTENANT PORTUONDO. So how can it be done? I want to know about this story. Would you consent to tell me all about it, if I let you have all of these? *(Holds out the letters.)*

MARIA CELIA. That would certainly compromise you, if you let me have all the letters.

LIEUTENANT PORTUONDO. You're right. But I can always read them to you.

MARIA CELIA. Then you don't want any evidence either. It has to be a clean crime.

LIEUTENANT PORTUONDO. Well, if you want to put it that way — I'm willing to read you the letters.

MARIA CELIA. I have more to lose than you do. You know that.

LIEUTENANT PORTUONDO. Why don't you think about it. You don't have to give me an answer now. Good day, compañera! *(He exits.)*
MARIA CELIA. *(In a loud voice.)* Sofia, are you there? *(Sofia comes out.)* Were you listening? Did you see all those letters? Did you see the whole pack? Hundreds of them.
SOFIA. I knew Antonio hadn't forgotten you. I knew. *(Lights fade to black.)*

Scene 2

THE BEDSPREADS OF DESIRE

Daytime. Soft, grayish white lights. It is raining outside. Maria Celia is reciting a letter to her husband.

MARIA CELIA. "My dear love: It's no longer a secret, the Ministry is holding up your letters. Every part of me, even my fury and rancor, is being registered and kept in a file. Now they're keeping your letters to document the weight of my heart. Today when I woke up and washed my face ... " *(Touches her face.)* "I thought that perhaps when you see me again, I'll be less than you expected, that you'll find me less beautiful. I'm thirty-six years old and I feel my life is evaporating in front of me, that I'm rotting and decaying in this house ... It's the thought of you, the strength of your eyes that brings the precipitation of life ... I kiss you all over, Maria Celia ... " *(Lights up on Sofia knitting.)*
SOFIA. We're almost out of the good yarn.
MARIA CELIA. What's wrong with this other yarn?
SOFIA. It's tough on my hands. It's like steel wool for scouring pots. You start weaving and purling with that thing and you'll end up with minced meat for hands.
MARIA CELIA. That's the only yarn we have left.
SOFIA. I have to protect my hands.
MARIA CELIA. Use a pair of gloves. If we don't knit there won't be any bedspreads. And if there's no bedspreads, what are we going to give Cirilo to sell?

17

SOFIA. It's days like this I could play the piano the whole day.

MARIA CELIA. I bet. You tell me that every day.

SOFIA. I can't play it anymore. The piano is falling apart.

MARIA CELIA. What about the permit you got to have it tuned?

SOFIA. I sent for a piano tuner — hasn't shown up.

MARIA CELIA. Give it some time.

SOFIA. Look at my hands, veins starting to show up from all this knitting. That's always been my fear. On men the veins look good. On men yes — because it makes them look strong and virile, like their plumbing works well and lots of blood flows through all their parts. I hate these needles. I hate all this knitting.

MARIA CELIA. I know. You tell me every time we knit.

SOFIA. Oscarito had lots of veins like a Roman aqueduct. Everywhere. I loved how they showed his strength. All the rivers from his heart. Oh, I wish I had a glass of rum with ice. A man … A man, is what I wish I had … I loved doing it when it rained. (Stretches.)

MARIA CELIA. You sound like a cat in heat.

SOFIA. Take a break for God's sake! I don't know where you get all that energy, when all we had to eat were eggs and mangoes.

MARIA CELIA. I'm tired but I keep at it. I keep at it.

SOFIA. If that lieutenant comes again you should ask him if he could get us something to eat.

MARIA CELIA. I told you I'm not going to ask him for food.

SOFIA. Why not? He could make life easier for us.

MARIA CELIA. No. I've been thinking of having him read me the letters and that's all.

I'm not going to give him any papers. I'm just going to tell him the story.

SOFIA. I wouldn't do it. He'll find something in it. It always happens.

MARIA CELIA. What could he possibly find? It's a simple love story, for God's sake!

SOFIA. He could testify against you. You keep me out of it.

MARIA CELIA. Keep you out of it and you want me to ask him for food!

SOFIA. Well, we have it bad as it is. I don't want anything else to do with your writing.

MARIA CELIA. I can't believe the things that come out of your mouth! You might as well turn me in.

SOFIA. I can't go back to the prison! Not back there, you hear me

18

… I'd rather be in a hole, underground, full of worms. Every night I have nightmares about that place. I wake up out of breath, like a lost animal …

MARIA CELIA. Forget I said anything. Do you remember when you were playing that song on the piano?

SOFIA. Which one?

MARIA CELIA. "La Savane." *(The music of Gottschalk is heard.)* I'd never heard it that way before. The whole music … I felt as if I had to leave my body. I went to the sea. Next minute, I was writing about this man and this woman in the marina. The story had gotten inside me like a sickness. For three days I stayed up at night writing.

SOFIA. Are you the woman in this story?

MARIA CELIA. No.

SOFIA. And him?

MARIA CELIA. He's like the man next door.

SOFIA. The man next door? Why him?

MARIA CELIA. I don't know. It all came to me that day.

The woman in the story goes to visit him at the marina when he's on duty. She always tells him that she wants to know about the sea … She wants to learn from him. The first night she goes to him, she asks if he eats alone, and he tells her that he does. She tells him it's sad to see men having dinner alone. A person should never eat alone. She asks him if she could cook for him. That they could have dinner together overlooking the sea.

SOFIA. Does he accept?

MARIA CELIA. He's not allowed to receive visitors when he's on duty. But she tells him that she wouldn't be a visitor, she'd only come to bring him food.

SOFIA. That'd be something I would say. And I would show up to see him even if he said no. I'd show up in a white dress.

MARIA CELIA. She wears a white dress.

SOFIA. Maybe a long blue scarf, to go with the sea, white sandals and a parasol.

MARIA CELIA. It's nighttime, Sofie. Why would she have a parasol?

SOFIA. That's true. You said it was nighttime. I'm sorry. You took me there with the story. *(Laughs.)* — Do you realize this is going to be another summer that we won't be able to go to the sea?

MARIA CELIA. Yes. I know.

SOFIA. I was sitting there with him at the marina with a picnic basket. My feet dangling from the pier … And me occasionally dipping my toes in the water, then looking at him.

MARIA CELIA. They meet on a tower, Sofie. A glass tower and it's not a picnic.

SOFIA. Go on. Don't mind me. I'm making your story into something else.

MARIA CELIA. Now I forgot where I was.

SOFIA. The glass tower.

MARIA CELIA. Yes, the glass tower surrounded by blue boats … Fishermen retrieving their nets from the sea. Seagulls.

SOFIA. Yes, lots of seagulls.

MARIA CELIA. The woman walks by the sea taking puffs from her cigarette, leaving smoke behind like a steamship. She climbs the stairs to the glass tower. She goes to see him, with her purse full of bread, rice, plantains, beans, boiled eggs, avocados, guava marmalade, napkins, forks, spoons, salt and pepper. A whole restaurant in her little bag.

SOFIA. That should be the name of the story: "Picnic by the Light of the Moon." I guess you can tell him all about it. What could be wrong with a picnic in a marina? But don't show him any writing.

VICTOR MANUEL. *(Offstage.)* Sofia … *(Both sisters look at each other.)*

SOFIA. Someone called my name. *(There's a knock at the door.)*

VICTOR MANUEL. *(Offstage.)* Sofia …

MARIA CELIA. Who is it?

VICTOR MANUEL. *(Offstage.)* Victor Manuel.

MARIA CELIA. Who?

VICTOR MANUEL. *(Offstage.)* Victor Manuel … I came to take a look at the piano. *(There is a pause. The two sisters look at each other again.)*

SOFIA. Yes … Yes … Coming … Coming … It's the piano tuner … The piano tuner … And me looking like a mess! Do I look all right?

MARIA CELIA. Open the door …

VICTOR MANUEL. *(Offstage.)* Open up … It's raining up a storm out here. *(Sofia rushes to the door. She fixes her hair a little and looks down at her clothes to see if she's presentable. She opens the door. Victor Manuel enters.)* What a storm … What a storm … It's a monsoon out there. *(Notices Sofia. Reaches out for her hand.)* Polita sent me here with this permit. She told me the piano needs tuning. *(He takes out a handkerchief.)* Which one is Sofia?

SOFIA. Me. I'm Sofia.

VICTOR MANUEL. I'm Victor Manuel.

MARIA CELIA. And I'm Maria Celia, her sister. *(He shakes her hand.)*

VICTOR MANUEL. At your service, compañera.

SOFIA. *(Stares at him. Becomes nervous. Awkward pause.)* The piano is right here. We didn't know you were coming. *(Uncovers the piano.)* My sister covered it as if it was a child. *(He looks at her.)* Humidity!

VICTOR MANUEL. *(Plays the piano. Then plays individual keys.)* Yes, it sounds bad. *(Key.)* Yes, bad. *(Key.)* Bad. *(Key.)* Bad. *(Key.)* It buzzes a little. Hear that … *(Key.)* I'll have to check the soundboard and the ribs. *(Takes out a flashlight from pocket. Inspects underneath the piano.)* When was the last time you had the piano tuned?

SOFIA. I guess more than two years ago. *(Looks at Maria Celia.)*

VICTOR MANUEL. Neglect ruins a piano, compañera. It's in real bad shape. When a piano is neglected it dies. It's like a plant, a tree. When you don't water a tree it withers away. *(Continues talking as he inspects the inside of the piano.)* I always say there should be mandatory rules for the use of pianos. If they are not being played … if they're not being put to good use, they should be donated to schools, hospitals, recreational parks. The Interior Ministry should intervene in this matter. Take inventory of all the pianos in the city, number them all and place them into categories: "The so-and-so family, living at such-and-such address makes use of their piano; the so-and-so family, at this other address uses the piano for family pictures and ashtrays." That's the only way we're going to get rid of the old system of using pianos for decoration. The old way of showing wealth and social class; through a piano in the living room.

MARIA CELIA. We're not bourgeois, compañero, if that's what you're implying.

VICTOR MANUEL. I'm talking to myself, compañera. I'm talking to myself. *(To Sofia now.)* There's some rust and corrosion on the metal parts. Some of the felt has to be changed … Some of the wires have to be replaced. You also have to change some of the wood in the bottom … See in there …

SOFIA. What's wrong with it?

VICTOR MANUEL. It's rotting. It looks like water got inside the piano.

MARIA CELIA. The dogs got in here, wrecked the whole place, stole things when the house got closed up. It's a good thing they didn't take an ax and chop it to pieces.

SOFIA. Maria Celia … please … *(To Victor Manuel.)* So what

21

should we do? Can you fix it?

VICTOR MANUEL. Well I suppose I can fix some things. As far as the wood in the bottom, that would mean dismantling some parts and having them custom-made. That will mean sending the piano to a repair place, where they can do that kind of work.

SOFIA. Where is this place?

VICTOR MANUEL. The only one I know is in the Oriente.

SOFIA. Well, if it needs to be sent there ...

MARIA CELIA. That's like saying the Himalayas. It would cost a fortune. We don't have that kind of money. — Can't you fix it somehow and make it sound pretty again?

VICTOR MANUEL. Well, I can certainly try. I'm just telling you about the major problems.

MARIA CELIA. You haven't told us how much you'll charge us.

VICTOR MANUEL. Twenty ...

MARIA CELIA. Twenty? That's a lot of money.

VICTOR MANUEL. That's how much I charge.

MARIA CELIA. Ten pesos. That's how much we can afford.

VICTOR MANUEL. Compañera, that's not enough to buy a can of sardines. How about five dollars? ... Five if you have dollars.

MARIA CELIA. We don't have dollars, and that's too much money for just pulling a couple of strings.

VICTOR MANUEL. *(Starts placing his tools in his bag.)* Well, that takes care of that. Perhaps I should leave. You're wasting my time ... And time is money. Money you won't spare. Money you don't have.

SOFIA. No ... Please. Don't leave. Wait one second. *(Sofia exits. Victor Manuel looks at Maria Celia.)*

VICTOR MANUEL. Where is she going? What is she going to do? I can't be wasting my time. I have other appointments. With all the celebrations for the Pan–American games, everybody wants their pianos tuned. You know it's the big event this year. Parties everywhere. There's people here from all over the world. — I'm sorry. Here I am carrying on and you stuck in this house ...

MARIA CELIA. It's all right, compañero. It's all right ...

VICTOR MANUEL. It's a shame what happened to you and your sister. You know, I've read some of your stories. The one about the woman who walks into the sea. I never thought the books were ... You know ...

MARIA CELIA. What?

VICTOR MANUEL. I mean ... The books ... It's a shame you started writing other kinds of material.

MARIA CELIA. What are you trying to get at, compañero?

VICTOR MANUEL. I mean … The … The new material … Your new stories. Your views, compañera. How you changed your opinion about the revolution.

MARIA CELIA. Is this an interrogation, compañero?

VICTOR MANUEL. No, of course not. Why would you say that?

MARIA CELIA. Then why all the little questions?

VICTOR MANUEL. I'm … Compañera please, I didn't mean to pry. Polita asked me to come and tune the piano … She gave me this permit.

MARIA CELIA. Anybody can say that, compañero. Anybody can grab a doctor's bag like yours …

VICTOR MANUEL. Now look! … Look, I can show you my identity card.

MARIA CELIA. What identity card? The government can fabricate those in a blink. How do I know you don't have a recording machine inside your doctor's bag, under your shirt?

VICTOR MANUEL. *(Opens the bag, furiously.)* Look … I don't … I don't … *(Shows her the bag and drops it on the floor. He opens his shirt and shows her his belly.)* Look … You can see … I have nothing under my shirt. *(Maria Celia doesn't look. Sofia enters with a shoebox.)* You want to look inside my pants? You want to see inside my pants? *(Starts to unfasten his pants.)*

SOFIA. What's going on?

VICTOR MANUEL. *Your sister wants to look inside my pants!* She says I'm an informer. Now here's my identity card. So, have I wasted my time by coming here or are you going to tune the piano?

SOFIA. Yes, of course. Maria Celia, please …

MARIA CELIA. We can afford only ten pesos. That's all we can afford. *(Maria Celia exits. Sofia looks at Victor Manuel.)*

SOFIA. *(Kneels down and opens the shoebox.)* I wanted to know if these shoes fit you. They're new. They belonged to my father. I thought this would make up for the rest of the money we don't have.

VICTOR MANUEL. *(Closes his eyes in disbelief.)* Ave Maria purisima!

SOFIA. Please … These are almost brand new. If the shoes don't fit, you can always sell them. *(Victor Manuel is trying to control himself. He brings his hand to his forehead as if he is trying to make sense of the whole situation. Sofia is now trying to take off his shoes.)* Please try them on.

VICTOR MANUEL. What are you doing?

SOFIA. What size do you wear? *(Gently tries to lift up his foot.)* I think these are a nine-and-a-half. Is that your size?

VICTOR MANUEL. No thank you, compañera. I wear a nine. Don't touch …

SOFIA. They'll fit you. These are nine-and-a-half. *(Trying to take off his shoes.)*

VICTOR MANUEL. Please, compañera don't … Please lady, don't … Please … Don't touch … My feet are ticklish … *(Tries to keep from laughing.)* Don't … *(Laughs.)* … Don't touch my feet, please … *(Tries on the shoes.)* I can put them on by myself! … I never let anybody touch my feet!

SOFIA. How do they fit?

VICTOR MANUEL. The left one feels …

SOFIA. Good leather.

VICTOR MANUEL. Well … I … I don't … *(Feels the comfort of the shoes.)* They actually … I … I mean … I can actually use a new pair of shoes. *(He's walking around the room to get a feel for the shoes.)* You have nothing to worry about … We'll give the piano a quick fix. The rest can be solved later. If a 1956 Chevy can run with Soviet parts, I can make this piano sound like a concert grand. *(Goes for the bag and opens it. There is a knock at the door. Victor Manuel looks at Sofia. Sofia is motionless.)*

LIEUTENANT PORTUONDO. *(Offstage.)* Can't you see the puddle, jerk! The streets aren't just for cars. *(Knocks again.)* Maria Celia … *(One more knock. Sofia goes to open the door. Lieutenant Portuondo comes in. He speaks rapidly as he takes off his raincoat. He holds a package. Straightening his clothes.)* — What a storm out there! We'll be swimming like fish by the time September gets here … *(Opens a paper bag.)* I brought some food, maybe it got all wet. *(The Lieutenant looks up and notices Victor Manuel. He's surprised to see him. He acts formally.)*

SOFIA. He's tuning the piano.

LIEUTENANT PORTUONDO. Can I see your identity card, compañero?

SOFIA. He's got a permit. He's got a permit from one of the inspectors to tune the piano.

VICTOR MANUEL. *(Shows him the permit.)* Just servicing the piano, compañero. Just here for work. *(Maria Celia enters the room.)*

SOFIA. The lieutenant is here to see you, Maria Celia.

MARIA CELIA. Good afternoon, Lieutenant.

LIEUTENANT PORTUONDO. Good afternoon, compañera.

Thank you, compañero. *(Gives him back the card.)*

MARIA CELIA. Come this way, Lieutenant. *(The Lieutenant and Maria Celia move to the left of the stage. The lights shift to this area.)* Did you think we hired a piano tuner without a permit from the inspectors?

LIEUTENANT PORTUONDO. Just doing my job, compañera. *(Giving her the bag.)* I brought you some food. I know it's hard to get food nowadays.

MARIA CELIA. That's kind of you, Lieutenant.

LIEUTENANT PORTUONDO. Also brought you these books, thought you might like to read them. *(Gives her the books.)* Simone de Beauvoir. Have you read her?

MARIA CELIA. Not this one.

LIEUTENANT PORTUONDO. Good. Now you have a book to read.

MARIA CELIA. And this book on Perestroika?

LIEUTENANT PORTUONDO. What about it?

MARIA CELIA. Why are you giving me this book? Are you testing me, Lieutenant?

LIEUTENANT PORTUONDO. No. Not at all. You're too suspicious, compañera. Don't you like Perestroika? Didn't you and all your artist friends write a manifesto about Perestroika?

MARIA CELIA. It got me in prison. I have this book.

LIEUTENANT PORTUONDO. Then I'll take it back.

MARIA CELIA. Wasn't it also taken off the shelves? I had to buy it from someone off the streets — exchanged a whole bag of rice for it.

LIEUTENANT PORTUONDO. That's almost a month of rice on your table.

MARIA CELIA. It's food for thought, Lieutenant. What we've forgotten in this island — to feed the mind. The fact that there are revolutions within revolutions. Are you recording what I'm saying? Is this why you brought these books, for me to run my mouth, and see if I've gone through *political rehabilitation?*

LIEUTENANT PORTUONDO. No. Not at all. On the contrary, I'm giving them to you because I thought you would like them. The one with the blue cover, this poet always writes about the sea, like you. I'll pretend I never gave them to you. I'm not a demon, compañera. I hope with time you'll learn to trust me. See, I trust you, already. *(Pulls out a letter from his pocket.)* I brought you a letter from your husband. I can read you part of it. Full letter if you decide to go ahead with the agreement. Would you like me to read you some?

MARIA CELIA. If you like. *(He looks at her. He opens the letter. She closes her eyes. Piano music swells, perhaps "The Waltz of the Shadows" by Lecuona.* Lights fade on Maria Celia and the Lieutenant. Lights slowly come up on the other side of the room. Victor Manuel is playing the piano. Sofia stands next to him lost in the music. After a while the song finishes.)*

SOFIA. What is it about that song? It just goes right to your soul. Why isn't this kind of music played on the radio? Why are we neglecting it?

VICTOR MANUEL. Oh, I don't neglect it. It's my favorite song. I play it all the time.

SOFIA. You do. But try playing it in public and people will say that you're bourgeois and sentimental … We don't play Lecuona because he was too romantic, Gershwin because he was American, Chopin because he was European. It's like everything old reeks of death. But how can one talk about these things, Victor Manuel?

VICTOR MANUEL. Well … I … I … I don't know … I.

SOFIA. Does it make you uncomfortable to talk about it?

VICTOR MANUEL. No … No … I play what I like in my house. I play this kind of music all the time. It's what I love. I don't know about other people but I still play it.

SOFIA. How come I never met you before?

VICTOR MANUEL. Oh, I don't know, I used to work at Carrion's piano store, before it burned down.

SOFIA. Yes … I remember when it happened, couldn't walk through the street after the fire. I couldn't bear to see all those melted pianos.

VICTOR MANUEL. Well, I should be running along. I really ought to be going. It's raining less now …

SOFIA. Please, stay with me a while longer. It's not every day I get to talk about the music I love. And sometimes, you never know who you can talk to. But you … My sister says I'm a fool because I trust any person who comes in here and stands in front of me … Because I speak my mind … Because I haven't lost the habit of saying things the way they're meant to be said … When you came here I thought … I thought …

VICTOR MANUEL. That I came to interrogate you …

SOFIA. You talked about the inventory of pianos. For a moment I thought you were going to …

VICTOR MANUEL. Take away the piano? No. I wouldn't. I

---

* See Special Note on Songs and Recordings on copyright page.

wouldn't do that to you.

SOFIA. *(Touches the piano.)* More than ninety years living in this house. Part of the family. My mother played it, my grandfather. He's like an old uncle. Probably the only one who still takes me out for a walk. Would you come back? *(Sofia holds his hand.)* Why don't you come back tomorrow?

VICTOR MANUEL. Look, I'd ... I'd like to ... But I don't know ... You and your sister ... This permit ...

SOFIA. You can always say you haven't finished tuning the piano. You have a permit.

VICTOR MANUEL. I mean ... I wouldn't know ... It's difficult ... It's risking ...

SOFIA. *(There are tears in her eyes.)* I understand.

VICTOR MANUEL. Look, I would like to. I like talking to you. *(Pause. Gently lifts up her chin.)* Please, you're making me feel ...

SOFIA. *(More contained.)* It's all right. I understand. *(Silence. He gathers some of his instruments and places them inside his bag. He looks at her.)*

VICTOR MANUEL. How about next week, I'll be less busy. The end of the games. I'll try to come.

SOFIA. All right. *(She kisses him.)*

VICTOR MANUEL. Tuesday then. *(He walks to the doorway. Then turns to her and waves goodbye. Lights change to Maria Celia sitting on a chair. The Lieutenant stands behind her.)*

MARIA CELIA. Would you read me part of another letter, Lieutenant?

LIEUTENANT PORTUONDO. If you want. *(He looks at her. He opens another letter and begins to read.)* "My dear love: A few moments ago I woke up, and walked to the store to buy writing paper, and I stopped by the bay. I stood there facing the water thinking of you."

MARIA CELIA. Please, read slower ... *(He looks at her. Maria Celia closes her eyes.)*

LIEUTENANT PORTUONDO. "I remembered how much you like to sit by the seawall and write for hours. The whole blue landscape had me holding your arms, your whole body once again. How I love your skin, your smell ... "

MARIA CELIA. Slower ...

LIEUTENANT PORTUONDO. How much slower do you want me to read?

MARIA CELIA. Just a little slower if you're not going to read me the whole thing. *(Closes her eyes to listen.)*

LIEUTENANT PORTUONDO. "I spent a couple of weeks in Sweden. I wonder if you got my postcard. I bought you a beautiful book on butterflies. I know how much you like them. Such a long time since I heard from you last. I've been in absolute torture for months now, but I don't let the dogs eat away at my hopes to see you again. I go nuts counting every day and week that goes by, and I just want the moment to come when I can have you free." *(No longer reading the letter, but looking at her.)* I close my eyes and try to imagine that day, when I can undress you like the first time and discover you all over again. Enter every secret place in your body. I want to make love for weeks and months, make up for all the lost time.

MARIA CELIA. You can stop now. *(He pretends to be reading.)* You can stop.

LIEUTENANT PORTUONDO. Are you all right, compañera?

MARIA CELIA. Yes.

LIEUTENANT PORTUONDO. Would you tell me a little bit of your story? *(There is a pause. She looks at him.)*

MARIA CELIA. It begins with the sultry months of summer. The man from the marina would call the woman and tell her not to come, that it'd be impossible for her to visit him. He had to be up on his feet keeping an eye out for lost ships. But the woman would disregard the calls, and show up to see him. She had thieves come to the marina and steal boats while she was upstairs in the tower. The rain, the storms made it easier to steal the boats. She'd tell the man about the foghorns, how the sound would make her sad. The wailing of the ships out there in the middle of the sea, and him in the tower alone like those ships ... She'd get the urge to go — That's all for now.

LIEUTENANT PORTUONDO. *(Folds the letter.)* Your husband is mad about you.

MARIA CELIA. He misses me.

LIEUTENANT PORTUONDO. I don't blame him. I would miss you too, if I were him. Have a good afternoon, compañera. *(The Lieutenant exits. The stage is fully lit now. Maria Celia is sitting on the sofa. Sofia runs to her.)*

SOFIA. Maria Celia, what did he bring us?

MARIA CELIA. *(Lost in thought.)* He read me part of a letter. I wish you could've heard him read it to me. For a moment I thought Antonio was in the room.

SOFIA. What did he have to say?

MARIA CELIA. Oh Sofie, you know the secret codes Antonio uses in his letters, the butterflies ...
SOFIA. Yes.
MARIA CELIA. He's been to Sweden.
SOFIA. Sweden?
MARIA CELIA. Yes. He's trying to find us political asylum there. He said he bought me a book on butterflies and that's what it means. He's still trying to get us out ...
SOFIA. So when did he say?
MARIA CELIA. The lieutenant didn't read me the whole thing.
SOFIA. Why not?
MARIA CELIA. There was probably information they don't want me to know. *(Pause.)* If I tell the lieutenant about my new writing, I want you to be in the room when he reads me the letters. I want you to be a witness.
SOFIA. Anything you want.
MARIA CELIA. Sooner than we think, tear down these walls and walk out of this house. Soon we'll be free. *(The music of Lecuona plays, perhaps "Andalucia."* Lights fade to black.)*

End of Act One

* See Special Note on Songs and Recordings on copyright page.

ACT TWO

Scene 1

WAITING FOR HIM ON TOP OF MY ROOF

Evening. As the lights start to dim, we hear music. Lights slowly come up on Sofia sitting on a chair. She wears a simple colorful dress. Maria Celia stands behind her combing her hair. Sofia is applying lipstick and looks into a small compact mirror. Maria Celia's mind wanders to her letter writing while she combs her sister's hair.

MARIA CELIA. "My dear love: I write to you in my mind, on my skin, even when I go about doing housework. Tonight Sofie has invited to dinner the man who tuned the piano — not that we can afford another dish on our table, but we'll have a visitor for a change." *(Sofia gets up and climbs upstairs to the roof. She stares into the distance waiting for Victor Manuel. Maria Celia walks around the room with a cloth dusting the sofa and the piano.)* "There are fewer and fewer products in the markets these days. We're running out of everything. We use milk of magnesia for deodorant. Soon we'll be out of lipstick and have to use beet juice to color our lips. I probably sound vain, because lipstick isn't necessary, but it's good to add a touch of red to the face for those blue days."

SOFIA. Maria Celia ... I think I see him coming ... Warm up the food ... He's walking down the street ...

MARIA CELIA. *(In a loud voice.)* Shouldn't I wait till he's actually here? This is the third time I've warmed up the food.

SOFIA. I think it's him walking this way ...

MARIA CELIA. Are you sure this time? It's almost nine-thirty now.

SOFIA. It's got to be him.

MARIA CELIA. Just come down, Sofie ... Come down ...

SOFIA. Wait ... First I want to see ...

MARIA CELIA. You've been up and down from that roof the

30

whole night.

SOFIA. He's crossing the street now …

MARIA CELIA. Is it him?

SOFIA. *(Climbs down from the roof and enters the house.)* You're right, he's not coming … It wasn't him.

MARIA CELIA. Oh Sofie, maybe something happened. Don't get that way. Maybe he went to one of the games. You know how men are, they are like children when it comes to sports. Maybe he's afraid of being seen here. Come on, cheer up … You and I will have dinner. I'm going to play a record, we'll have a good time. I want you to dance with me. Come on … *(Maria Celia goes behind the sofa and plays a fast Cuban song.)* Dance with me … Dance … *(The music livens up the mood. Maria Celia starts dancing with Sofia … Sofia gives in to the dance, and the sisters start showing off their best steps and turns. They laugh, enjoying their dancing. There is a knock at the door. Maria Celia turns off the music. There is another knock. Sofia fixes her hair and clothes and goes to open the door, expecting the piano tuner. Lieutenant Portuondo enters dressed in a summer suit.)*

LIEUTENANT PORTUONDO. Listening to music?

SOFIA. Yes … We … We were … *(Pause.)*

LIEUTENANT PORTUONDO. Celebrating the end of the Pan–American Games?

SOFIA and MARIA CELIA. No …

MARIA CELIA. We're … just … just listening to some records …

LIEUTENANT PORTUONDO. You're all dressed up this evening.

MARIA CELIA. *(Nervously.)* We are … Aren't we? … Get tired of the same clothes.

LIEUTENANT PORTUONDO. I brought some rum, thought maybe you'd like to have a drink with me.

SOFIA. No. You'll have to excuse me, Lieutenant, I'm going to bed.

MARIA CELIA. Stay up a while longer.

LIEUTENANT PORTUONDO. Have a drink with us. *(To Maria Celia.)* Would you bring some glasses? It's a night for celebration. We won over seventy medals in the games. We beat the Americans in almost everything. Can you believe it?

SOFIA. Our radio is broken, Lieutenant. We don't get any news. We don't know what's happening out there in the world.

LIEUTENANT PORTUONDO. You should give it to me. I'll have it fixed. *(Maria Celia gives him the glasses. He opens the bottle.)*

MARIA CELIA. No. You don't have to, Lieutenant.

LIEUTENANT PORTUONDO. I'll fix it for you. I know someone who fixes radios. *(Pours the rum.)* Sweet poison, this rum. Everywhere there are tourists drinking tonight, burning their guts out. Can you hear the drums? They make the island come alive. They release things from inside people. *(Raises glass.)* Salud.

MARIA CELIA. Salud. *(Smells the rum, takes a sip.)*

SOFIA. Salud.

MARIA CELIA. I haven't had rum in so long, forgot what it tastes like.

SOFIA. Me, too.

LIEUTENANT PORTUONDO. Well, drink up. I brought a whole bottle.

SOFIA. It seems like the whole island is out tonight. How come you're not out celebrating?

LIEUTENANT PORTUONDO. Because I wanted to see the two of you.

SOFIA. An odd place to visit. Not even the moon comes to this house.

LIEUTENANT PORTUONDO. Well, that's the moon for you. I like visiting you.

MARIA CELIA. If it weren't this late I'd go out into the patio and pull a few mint leaves from our plants. A little mint would give the rum the finishing touch.

LIEUTENANT PORTUONDO. What's the matter, you're afraid of the darkness? Tell me where the mint plant is. I'll pull a few leaves.

MARIA CELIA. No. It's not good to disturb the plants at this hour. It's an old African belief, respect for the night, the plants … Our mother used to say:

MARIA CELIA and SOFIA. *(Laughing.)* "Never ask a tree for fruit at night, because the whole wilderness sleeps after sundown."

LIEUTENANT PORTUONDO. You fascinate me, compañera.

SOFIA. That was our mother, Lieutenant.

LIEUTENANT PORTUONDO. Well I think the two of you are fascinating.

SOFIA. No. Not like she was.

MARIA CELIA. She was a lovely woman, Lieutenant.

SOFIA. Yes, she was.

MARIA CELIA. Every time she entered the patio out there, all the plants rejoiced in her presence.

SOFIA. And here in this room, every afternoon she'd sit to play the piano and the whole neighborhood would quiet down to listen to her music.

LIEUTENANT PORTUONDO. So talent runs in the family, you and your mother played the piano and Maria Celia writes ... How about your father?

SOFIA. He was an accountant ...

MARIA CELIA. Someone had to do the numbers.

SOFIA. Oh, we can tell you stories about our family —

MARIA CELIA. Every day we discover things about Mamá for the first time —

SOFIA. Why her room was on the east side of the house —

MARIA CELIA. Because she loved the morning light.

SOFIA. Why she used to write prayers on the soles of our shoes.

MARIA CELIA. Why she had her own views about the revolution.

LIEUTENANT PORTUONDO. She was a revolutionary?

SOFIA. Maybe not the kind you would like.

MARIA CELIA. We've always been revolutionary, Lieutenant. The whole family.

LIEUTENANT PORTUONDO. So why did your father leave the country?

SOFIA. He felt he couldn't speak his mind.

LIEUTENANT PORTUONDO. I see. I suppose it can be difficult sometimes.

SOFIA. You suppose right enough.

LIEUTENANT PORTUONDO. My old man ... He left just like your father.

SOFIA. He did.

LIEUTENANT PORTUONDO. Got fed up one day and said, "This isn't going anywhere." Got tired of waiting. He wanted to take me with him.

SOFIA. You?

LIEUTENANT PORTUONDO. Yes. But I was already in the military.

MARIA CELIA. I can't imagine you living up North.

LIEUTENANT PORTUONDO. Well sometimes I wonder what my life would've been like if I'd left. The poor man, ended up in some snowy town. Never married again after my mother died. He used to say he was old and didn't have any more heart left in him. — Was a good man, my father. Hard worker ... Had an old Buick, used to travel the whole island selling milk containers to farmers. I used to help him on the road. Many a time, I saw his eyes water, when an old bolero used to play on the radio, and I'd ask him, "Why you crying, Pipo?" And he'd say, "I just saw Pucha, your mother, through the mirror." And I'd turn around to look and there'd be no one on the backseat. And he'd keep on telling me, "Oh, I know she's there, I can smell her sweet powder." It used to give me the creeps.

MARIA CELIA. Why?

LIEUTENANT PORTUONDO. Knowing my father, he'd let go of the steering wheel and jump on the backseat with her. *(They laugh.)* More rum?

MARIA CELIA. Just a bit. *(The Lieutenant pours some rum in her glass.)*

LIEUTENANT PORTUONDO. You know, every time I come to this house I seem to forget the world. Something about you and your sister. You're different. *(Pours some rum in Sofia's glass.)*

SOFIA. I'm sure we are, especially now in Mamá's clothes.

LIEUTENANT PORTUONDO. No, what I'm talking about is something in the blood.

MARIA CELIA. In the blood?

LIEUTENANT PORTUONDO. Yes. What is it? What is that something that is passed on, that makes us who we are? I mean intelligence … Grace … You're pure … You are who you are, unlike me. I don't know what I'm saying … Ey, what would I know! I come from the middle of nowhere. A miserable town made of mud. Houses made of palm leaves. Dirt floor. No running water. I think people die there from looking at the cows. You know the only thing I liked about that place were the hurricanes. I loved the hurricanes. I was always waiting for the wind to blow hard enough and blow me away from there. *(Drinks. Sound of voices coming from the outside, firecrackers.)*

MARIA CELIA. What is that noise?

LIEUTENANT PORTUONDO. It must be the people going home from the stadium.

SOFIA. They sound happy and cheerful.

MARIA CELIA. They do. *(Pause.)* Did anybody see you come in here at this hour? There's always somebody keeping an eye on this house.

LIEUTENANT PORTUONDO. Don't worry. People know who I am.

MARIA CELIA. I'd be careful if I were you. It's not five o'clock in the afternoon.

LIEUTENANT PORTUONDO. Well, I wanted to see you, and that's all that matters. I'd like to get to know the two of you. I'd like for us to talk.

MARIA CELIA. Talk about what, Lieutenant?

LIEUTENANT PORTUONDO. I mean talk.

MARIA CELIA. We are talking, aren't we?

LIEUTENANT PORTUONDO. No, I mean … When are you going to trust me?

MARIA CELIA. Trust you how, Lieutenant?

LIEUTENANT PORTUONDO. How can I make you stop seeing me as the enemy?

MARIA CELIA. Being the enemy is not necessarily a bad thing. You probably know that more than I do. Lets you keep your resistance, your perspective in life.

LIEUTENANT PORTUONDO. And what's your perspective in life? How do you know it's any different than mine?

MARIA CELIA. Oh, come on, Lieutenant.

LIEUTENANT PORTUONDO. That isn't fair … You hardly know me.

SOFIA. I'm going upstairs to the roof … It seems like there are people dancing in the streets. I want to watch them from up there.

LIEUTENANT PORTUONDO. Have another drink with us?

SOFIA. No, you'll have to excuse me. *(Exits.)*

LIEUTENANT PORTUONDO. *(Pouring more rum in Maria Celia's glass.)* A little more rum. *(He refills his glass.)* Salud. *(He raises his glass. She doesn't toast, but stares him in the face. He smiles and drinks. He's amused by her control.)* You know, the more I get to know you, the more I understand your husband's letters.

MARIA CELIA. What do you mean?

LIEUTENANT PORTUONDO. This man would do anything to have you by his side. It's all here, in this letter.

MARIA CELIA. Do you always carry my husband's letters with you?

LIEUTENANT PORTUONDO. No. I brought you this letter tonight, because I thought you'd like to know about your husband's trip to Sweden.

MARIA CELIA. What about his trip?

LIEUTENANT PORTUONDO. I don't know. These lines may lend themselves to more than one interpretation, and you know very well what I mean. He talks about the photos he took in Sweden. Something about them looking sad and gray. What do you think that means?

MARIA CELIA. I don't know. They say those northern countries look sad and melancholy.

LIEUTENANT PORTUONDO. Are you sure that doesn't mean something else? He writes about several objects he bought on his trip. They seemed to have gotten lost in the mail … A painting, an old book on butterflies. Could this mean that he's not having any luck getting you out of this place? Was he trying to find you an asylum in Sweden?

MARIA CELIA. What are you after, Lieutenant? What do you want to know?! Just tell me. I mean, I'm standing here listening to you and I'm thinking, is this a new game? … Is it really his letter? Or is this some kind of new trial I'm supposed to endure?

LIEUTENANT PORTUONDO. Look, you can see for yourself. It's his handwriting. *(He shows her the letter, then folds it and places it in his pocket. Silence. A part of her seems to have left the room. She walks to the other side of the room. There are tears in her eyes.)*

MARIA CELIA. You should go, Lieutenant.

LIEUTENANT PORTUONDO. I'm sorry.

MARIA CELIA. Just go, please.

LIEUTENANT PORTUONDO. I want to try to help you, Maria Celia. Why won't you let me help you?

MARIA CELIA. What can you do? We both know what that letter is saying. You know everything about my life. That was my last hope. *(Her mind is somewhere else. But she takes refuge in the absurdity of the whole thing. With a faint smile.)* Well, what would Sofie and I do in Sweden. We would probably look like two out-of-season tropical palms.

LIEUTENANT PORTUONDO. I don't think you should leave the country once you're released from this house.

MARIA CELIA. I never thought exile was the answer. But what would I do here?

LIEUTENANT PORTUONDO. You are needed here, and I don't tell you this because you are standing in front of me and I have a couple of drinks in my head … Look, I'm all for change, just like you … That manifesto you wrote about Perestroika …

MARIA CELIA. It got me nowhere, Lieutenant!

LIEUTENANT PORTUONDO. It just wasn't the right time. But now … Look, the island is going to open up soon, just like the rest of the world … Things are going to change …

MARIA CELIA. Please, I prefer …

LIEUTENANT PORTUONDO. No, listen to me …

MARIA CELIA. I prefer not to talk about it … All I did was write the words "change" … "individual rights" … "a little more freedom" on a piece of paper and what happened?! All my writing became suspicious, a mob threw rocks at my door, two years in prison, and then I got locked up in my own house. So please just …

LIEUTENANT PORTUONDO. I believe in what you wrote, Maria Celia. I'm with you … *(Pause.)* You know, tonight I came here wanting — I was hoping for some kind of understanding between the two of us. You and I … We treat each other …

MARIA CELIA. I think I stopped trying to understand many things …

LIEUTENANT PORTUONDO. And so have I. I certainly don't try to understand why I'm here in this house. Why I'm willing to read you these letters. I gave up trying to understand. You know very well I'm risking my skin. *(For the first time he realizes this is a political confession and also a confession of the heart. Sofia comes down from the roof. She stays at a distance to listen to the conversation.)* I'd like to help you stop waiting. *(There is a pause. She looks at him.)*

MARIA CELIA. I love my husband, Lieutenant.

LIEUTENANT PORTUONDO. I know. And I love that about you. That's how I met you. I love everything about you … Your writing … Your mind … The way you think, how you see the world.

SOFIA. If you're leaving, Lieutenant, you should go out the back door. The head of the neighborhood committee is sitting on her doorstep.

LIEUTENANT PORTUONDO. That's all right, compañera. Thank you. Would you give me the radio before I go? I'd like to fix it for you.

SOFIA. If you insist. *(She hands him the radio.)*

LIEUTENANT PORTUONDO. Have a good night.

MARIA CELIA. Lieutenant …

LIEUTENANT PORTUONDO. Yes …

MARIA CELIA. Bring me a letter tomorrow and I want you to read me the whole thing. We'll go ahead with our arrangement.

LIEUTENANT PORTUONDO. Tomorrow then. *(Exits.)*

MARIA CELIA. Are you all right? You've been up and down the roof the whole night.

SOFIA. I walked all the way past Tito's house on top of the roof. I want to go out. I can't stand it here anymore. I just want out. *(The sound of drums fills the stage. Lights fade to black.)*

Scene 2

HER HUSBAND'S LETTER FOR A STORY

The lights start to slowly come up. Sofia enters with betel palm trees in terra-cotta containers.

SOFIA. Where do you want me to put these?

MARIA CELIA. *(Offstage.)* By the doorway.

SOFIA. What's gotten into you today?

MARIA CELIA. *(Offstage.)* We need some life in this house.

SOFIA. It would take more than these shrubs.

MARIA CELIA. *(Offstage.)* Do they look good there?

SOFIA. No. They look better next to the piano. *(Maria Celia enters with another plant. Sofia walks to the wall and presses her ear to listen. Maria Celia exits and returns with another palm tree and places it by the doorway.)* We haven't heard the man next door in more than two weeks. Not a sound from in there. You think something happened to him?

MARIA CELIA. He's probably busy working.

SOFIA. I miss listening to him. He's never been gone for so long. Maybe he's sick in the hospital.

MARIA CELIA. Ay, Sofia … Why would he be in the hospital? He's strong as a horse.

SOFIA. You're right, he's strong. He's built like a bull.

MARIA CELIA. Help me bring in the other pots.

SOFIA. I suppose the lieutenant will be coming this afternoon.

MARIA CELIA. I suppose he will.

SOFIA. And you'll want me to sit here.

MARIA CELIA. I was hoping you would.

SOFIA. "I was hoping," she says. I might as well be another plant in the room.

MARIA CELIA. I'll bring in the other plants. *(Exits.)*

SOFIA. That's fine. I'll do whatever you want me to do. Like always, until doomsday. *(There's a knock at the door.)* Oh God! It's probably him. *(She goes to open the door. The Lieutenant comes in.)* We weren't expecting you until much later.

LIEUTENANT PORTUONDO. Left work early today.

SOFIA. Maria Celia is out in the patio. This is her new plan for today, to fill the house with plants.

LIEUTENANT PORTUONDO. It looks good.

SOFIA. You think so? I can't even tell the difference. Everything looks the same to me in this place. Can I get you anything, Lieutenant?

LIEUTENANT PORTUONDO. No, thank you.

SOFIA. How are things out there in the *world?*

LIEUTENANT PORTUONDO. It's hot. The streets are burning from this heat.

SOFIA. Not any hotter than in this house. Have you been to the movies lately?

LIEUTENANT PORTUONDO. No, I haven't.

SOFIA. I used to love going to the movies, especially in the summer. It's a good place to escape the heat.

LIEUTENANT PORTUONDO. Yes, it is.

SOFIA. Oh, I wish you could get us a permit, Lieutenant.

LIEUTENANT PORTUONDO. What kind of permit do you want?

SOFIA. Something to go out of the house, even if it's just once a week.

MARIA CELIA. *(Entering with another plant.)* I think this bromeliad will look nice inside the house. *(Notices the Lieutenant.)*

SOFIA. I was just about to call you …

MARIA CELIA. Hello, Lieutenant!

LIEUTENANT PORTUONDO. Hello.

SOFIA. Give me the plant, I'll put it on the table. Sit here on the sofa, Lieutenant. I think I'd rather sit by the piano.

LIEUTENANT PORTUONDO. *(To Sofia.)* I imagine this is like the old days, when your friends used to gather here to read stories and poems.

SOFIA. No, it's not the same.

LIEUTENANT PORTUONDO. I'm sure there were more people and it was livelier.

SOFIA. Many more. This place was full of life before. Now everything has a sad stare … Every piece of furniture has a tag like an agony. Sometimes I think I'm going to go mad in this closed-up house. I spend so much time in this damned place.

MARIA CELIA. Well, perhaps we should start now, Sofie. *(Maria Celia turns to the Lieutenant.)* Lieutenant.

39

LIEUTENANT PORTUONDO. *(Takes out a letter and begins to read.)* "My dear Maria Celia: Your letter came yesterday and brought with it a garden of palm trees, the wind from your patio. The little place where you sit on the roof. Sometimes I can see you without seeing you, as if I were there next to you. I can picture what you do in the morning, at what time you have coffee, comb your hair, at what time you wash your face and undress." *(He looks at her.)* "Every day I dream about you, my love. I can feel your arms and legs wrapped around my body like before … Your skin soft, delicate, tender and hot … Your face madly alive when I am inside you … Your voice calling out, asking me to go further … To go as far as death … I'm holding your last letter in my hands now … Tonight I'll sleep inside you, my love. Please write to me soon. Antonio. P.S. I'm including a few jasmine flowers from the tree outside my window. They remind me of you."

MARIA CELIA. May I see the flowers? *(The Lieutenant gives her the three little dry flowers. She smells them. He looks at her. There is silence.)*

SOFIA. I … I feel … I feel as if I should do something. Maybe have something to read. So quiet all of a sudden. Maybe I could play the piano.

LIEUTENANT PORTUONDO. Yes. Play something.

SOFIA. How about this? You know this song? *(She begins to play a song like "Yo te quiero siempre" by Lecuona.* The Lieutenant walks toward the piano. He leaves the letter with Maria Celia. She's reading it now as she smells the flowers. Sofia immerses herself in her music. She looks at the Lieutenant as she plays. He stares at Maria Celia. Sofia turns her face to Maria Celia as she plays, then back to the Lieutenant. The Lieutenant lets himself be taken by the music, but his eyes always return to Maria Celia. Holding the flowers, Maria Celia walks upstage, to look at the light entering from a window. The Lieutenant watches her. Sofia closes her eyes, recoiling in the music. The Lieutenant walks toward Maria Celia. She is smelling the flowers, then hands them for him to smell. Sofia closes the piano and walks out of the room. Maria Celia and the Lieutenant turn toward Sofia. Maria Celia is about to go after her …)*

LIEUTENANT PORTUONDO. Don't go … *(Maria Celia remains still, looking in the direction of her sister. Lieutenant Portuondo comes closer to her. He touches her shoulder. He kisses her*

* See Special Note on Songs and Recordings on copyright page.

neck. He turns her face. He kisses her lips, her face and all over her neck and shoulders. He makes his way down her body. He's down on his knees now kissing her legs, pulling up her dress. Her back arches, then bends forward to him as if succumbing to the pull of pleasure. The two bodies have become one on the floor. The sound of nightfall drowns the whole moment into a gentle darkness. Then full darkness. The lights come up again. Maria Celia is lying on the floor with the Lieutenant telling him the story.)

MARIA CELIA. Then she moves around the room, like the light that enters slowly from the lighthouse. She changes the conversation. And slowly like the high tide that creeps in the afternoon, she brings the calm sea to the room. The whole room drowns in a blue glory. He no longer remembers the marine reports. He can only smell the wet air of the bay. His whole body becomes a vessel, a galleon. His open shirt, a flying sail in the wind navigating towards her open sea. *(Sofia enters the stage, but stays at a distance, watching.)*

LIEUTENANT PORTUONDO. So the woman in your story is responsible for the stolen boats. She distracts the man while she's upstairs in the tower. Does the woman love this man?

MARIA CELIA. I think she does. But she probably doesn't want to know this.

LIEUTENANT PORTUONDO. Is that why she's lying to him?

MARIA CELIA. Perhaps he's been lying, too. Maybe he knew the boats were being stolen all along, but he pretended not to know.

LIEUTENANT PORTUONDO. Why would he do that?

MARIA CELIA. So she could always come back to him. *(They kiss.)*

LIEUTENANT PORTUONDO. You're beautiful beyond anything I've seen in my life …

MARIA CELIA. I am? Tell me that again.

LIEUTENANT PORTUONDO. You're beautiful, beautiful, beautiful …

MARIA CELIA. You have awakened a hunger in me that starts from my feet to my hair, as if my mouth is again my own, my breathing … Like I'm tasting everything for the first time.

LIEUTENANT PORTUONDO. I want to know everything about you. I want to eat with you and shower with you …

MARIA CELIA. Are you as hungry as I am?

LIEUTENANT PORTUONDO. Yes, for you. *(Kisses her neck.)*

MARIA CELIA. No, wait. I think there's some mangoes left in the kitchen.

LIEUTENANT PORTUONDO. Messy fruit, the mango.

MARIA CELIA. Messy like you.

LIEUTENANT PORTUONDO. Let's eat it naked in your room. *(Maria Celia takes him by the hand. They exit. The sounds of the night fill the stage. The lights become darker. The scene moves deeper into the night as time passes. Sofia enters cautiously, holding a bundle of men's clothes. She wears a fedora hat. She drops the bundle of clothes on top of the sofa as she glances toward her sister's room. She listens for any sounds coming from there. She stands by the sofa and starts to disguise herself as a man. She puts on a pair of pants and shirt. She tucks her dress inside the pants. Maria Celia enters.)*

MARIA CELIA. Who's there? Who's there?

SOFIA. *(In a low voice.)* Shshhhhh ... Don't scream ... Don't be frightened it's me.

MARIA CELIA. Oh my God ... You gave me a fright. I was ... I thought someone ... I thought someone had gotten in ...

SOFIA. Shssh ... Go back to bed, it's still dark.

MARIA CELIA. What are you doing?

SOFIA. I couldn't sleep.

MARIA CELIA. Why are you dressing like a man?

SOFIA. I'm trying on Papi's clothes.

MARIA CELIA. What do you mean you're trying on Papi's clothes? Were you going out?

SOFIA. No.

MARIA CELIA. You're lying.

LIEUTENANT PORTUONDO. *(Offstage.)* Maria Celia ...

MARIA CELIA. *(In a loud voice to the Lieutenant.)* Coming ... *(To Sofia.)* Take off those clothes!

SOFIA. No.

MARIA CELIA. *(Starts taking off Sofia's shirt.)* Are you crazy?

SOFIA. *(Pulls away.)* I don't care what you say. I'm going out.

MARIA CELIA. If you get caught you're going back to prison. *(The Lieutenant enters the room but stays at a distance, watching.)*

SOFIA. The hell with you. Let go. *(Maria Celia lets go of her arm. Sofia takes the jacket and hat and runs off.)*

MARIA CELIA. *(In a low voice.)* Sofia ... Sofia ...

LIEUTENANT PORTUONDO. Maria Celia ... *(Maria Celia stays motionless. Pause. She turns to him.)*

MARIA CELIA. Would you keep this between us? — Please, Alejandro would you do that for me? *(He looks at her, then exits. Maria Celia remains alone. Lights fade to black.)*

Scene 3

COUNTING THE LOST STITCHES

The morning after Sofia's escape. Maria Celia and Sofia have been arguing. Lieutenant Portuondo enters holding a shirt.

LIEUTENANT PORTUONDO. Did anybody follow you?

SOFIA. I already told you. No … No.

LIEUTENANT PORTUONDO. Did you go into anyone's house?

SOFIA. No.

LIEUTENANT PORTUONDO. Where did you go then? Where?

SOFIA. I ran through the streets like a wild horse.

LIEUTENANT PORTUONDO. That's not what I asked you.

SOFIA. Then what do you want to know?

LIEUTENANT PORTUONDO. Did you talk to anybody?

SOFIA. Yes I talked to the sea, to the sky, to the cars and bicycles passing me by … Is that what you want to know? Now leave me in peace!

LIEUTENANT PORTUONDO. *(Completely enraged.)* Leave you in peace! Do you know what the fuck you did! …

SOFIA. *(Erupting all of a sudden.)* I know what I did and I don't need to be reminded! So you can stop looking at me as if I committed murder, because I'm not taking it back. If you're so interested … If you want to know what really happened to me out there, I had a good time! I sat by the seawall, felt the fresh air in my lungs. I watched people sitting in the park. A man came to me and said, "What a beautiful night." Felt like a human being again!

LIEUTENANT PORTUONDO. *(To Maria Celia.)* You know, I've about had it … You deal with your sister. I'm scared of what she might do next. *(He exits into the bedroom to get the rest of his clothes. Silence.)*

SOFIA. Maria Celia. *(Silence. Then almost in a hush.)* Look at me … I have to talk to you … Something big has happened in Russia … We have to talk …

MARIA CELIA. Talk. After what you did, do you expect me to talk to you?

43

SOFIA. Listen to me ...

MARIA CELIA. It's bad enough being stuck in this house with your foolish self!

SOFIA. And do you think I like being stuck in here with you?

MARIA CELIA. At least I don't do anything to jeopardize you.

SOFIA. Jeopardize me? You have him stay in here, and that's not putting me at risk ... *(The Lieutenant storms in.)*

LIEUTENANT PORTUONDO. Why don't you keep your mouth shut, when you've got nothing to say.

SOFIA. Bullshit, and you both know it! It sickens me to look at the two of you.

LIEUTENANT PORTUONDO. You walked out of this house, you piece — !

SOFIA. Oh, don't try to give me a guilty conscience! It's because of people like you ... It's because of her that I spent two years in prison ... Her rotten books ... Her friends and their literary meetings ... That damn letter they wrote about Perestroika ...

MARIA CELIA. You were the first to sign the letter. *(To the Lieutenant.)* She was the first to play music at the literary meetings, when Oscarito read his poems. That scoundrel she was in love with.

SOFIA. Hah! I should've left with him to Spain. *(Looks at the Lieutenant.)* He was a real man ... Don't I wish that I had him back in my life! Him and all the other men that came my way.

MARIA CELIA. He was an opportunist, who went off to Europe spouting information in all the papers about the two of us in prison. He got himself a job.

SOFIA. He was trying to get us amnesty.

MARIA CELIA. What amnesty? I don't see any amnesty.

SOFIA. At least he tried helping us. Not like him, who hasn't done anything to get us out.

LIEUTENANT PORTUONDO. *(Enraged.)* You know I should cut off your tongue!

SOFIA. *(Pushes him.)* Yes, kill me! Go ahead. I wish you would.

MARIA CELIA. *(Pulls her away.)* Sofia, stop! *(Pause.)*

LIEUTENANT PORTUONDO. You don't know what the fuck you've done! *(The Lieutenant storms out. Silence.)*

MARIA CELIA. *(Starts to knit.)* All your life begrudging me something.

SOFIA. Begrudging you what?! Why would I be jealous of you? Maybe your lieutenant is making it harder for us to get out. *(Maria Celia doesn't respond.)* Knit and purl, knit and purl ... I hate those

stupid needles! *(Takes her needles and throws them on the floor.)*
MARIA CELIA. Pick them up … *(Sofia stays motionless.)* You act like a child, rash and reckless … *(Maria Celia goes to pick up the needles.)* If there's one thing we can learn from all this knitting, it's that you have to go back where you left off … You have to pick up the lost stitches.
SOFIA. I've lost a whole life of stitches in this house. A whole life. That's what gets to me. So many days, gone … I could knit a bedspread for this whole island with all the lost days. I can't even remember where I left off living my own life. My own place in this mess! I'll never forget that day when Papi left the country. When he kissed us on the forehead and told us not to fall in love, not to get married, because he was going to send for us … As if love was a car one could stop with the touch of the brakes. For me time stopped. I felt my feet stop growing, my bones, my breasts, as if I had frozen in time, because I was saving myself for North America. It just feels like all my life I've been waiting and I haven't lived. You got to travel with your books. You got married, when you got tired of waiting. But me, stuck here. Stuck, piano lessons, a few students, taking care of Mamá. Stuck … Stuck … Stuck … And now stuck even more.
MARIA CELIA. Sofie please … *(Holds Sofia's arm, trying to console her.)*
SOFIA. No. Can't you see what you are doing?! Can't you see what you're getting yourself into with that man? He's not going to make it better for us. I've watched him … He got rid of all the inspectors who used to come to this house. He's the only one who comes here. Can't you see it spelled out on his forehead. Ownership! Everything about him screams out zookeeper.
MARIA CELIA. That's enough, Sofia! That's enough! *(There is a pause. Sofia looks at her a moment. Maria Celia is shaken by what Sofia has said.)*
SOFIA. Last night I heard a group of men talking about Russia. Something big has happened there, Maria Celia. They said the Soviet Union has broken apart, that it's over … Can you believe it! Thousands of people in the squares … That's what I heard … All over Moscow celebrating … Statues tumbling down … *(Maria Celia walks to another part of the room. She seems to be somewhere else, lost.)* Maybe something will happen here, too.
MARIA CELIA. Maybe.
SOFIA. One man was even talking about the new maps … He was

saying the world is going to seem bigger with all the changes. Can you imagine? Someone is out there sketching new maps of the world. *(Lights fade to black.)*

Scene 4

AFTER THE SOVIET COUP

The lights slowly come up on Sofia and Lieutenant Portuondo standing by the doorway.

LIEUTENANT PORTUONDO. Where's your sister? Did you tell her I came by earlier?

SOFIA. I did.

LIEUTENANT PORTUONDO. Did you tell her I wanted to talk to her?

SOFIA. I did. She said that she didn't think she'd be able to get up from bed. You look a little sick, too, Lieutenant. You haven't been sleeping well?

LIEUTENANT PORTUONDO. No.

SOFIA. Me neither. The summer heat is agonizing, isn't it?

LIEUTENANT PORTUONDO. Can I get your sister something?

SOFIA. She'll be fine. You must have a lot of work, Lieutenant … I mean, with everything that happened in Russia, you must be busy …

LIEUTENANT PORTUONDO. What about Russia?

SOFIA. I mean … So much has happened out there in the world. I mean the big revolt in Moscow … When I heard about it, I thought …

LIEUTENANT PORTUONDO. I'd like to talk to your sister. Why don't you call her?

SOFIA. I told you she's …

LIEUTENANT PORTUONDO. Call her … *(In a loud voice.)* Maria Celia. *(To Sofia.)* Go get her.

SOFIA. I told you she's not feeling well.

LIEUTENANT PORTUONDO. Go get her I said. *(Calling.)* Maria Celia. *(Sofia exits, then returns.)* Is she coming?

SOFIA. I suppose so. She's up on the roof. *(Maria Celia enters.)*

LIEUTENANT PORTUONDO. What's the matter with you?

MARIA CELIA. Sofie must have told you, I haven't been feeling well.

LIEUTENANT PORTUONDO. Sick? and you were up on the roof.

SOFIA. She needed some air.

LIEUTENANT PORTUONDO. Is it possible to have a word with you? *(Sofia exits. He looks at Maria Celia.)* For three days I've been coming here. I thought you didn't want to see me.

MARIA CELIA. Sofie told you — I haven't been feeling …

LIEUTENANT PORTUONDO. Do you need anything?

MARIA CELIA. No, thank you. *(She moves away from him.)*

LIEUTENANT PORTUONDO. Are you feeling better?

MARIA CELIA. No.

LIEUTENANT PORTUONDO. If you like, I can go and come back later. *(Pause.)*

MARIA CELIA. Did you fix my radio?

LIEUTENANT PORTUONDO. I haven't had time to go by the shop and pick it up.

MARIA CELIA. Would you get it for me?

LIEUTENANT PORTUONDO. Sure. I can pick it up tomorrow.

MARIA CELIA. It seems like the whole world is upside down.

LIEUTENANT PORTUONDO. Why do you say that?

MARIA CELIA. I can see the people from the roof. I can see through their faces … Their eyes elsewhere … Their minds wondering, questioning what happened in Russia.

LIEUTENANT PORTUONDO. This morning we had to arrest a boy.

MARIA CELIA. What did he do?

LIEUTENANT PORTUONDO. He was protesting … He climbed to the top of a street lamp. We couldn't get him to come down. He said he was going to electrocute himself. The crowd went wild. I couldn't do anything about it. *(Shakes his head.)* It was awful. He was just a boy, eleven or twelve.

MARIA CELIA. Do you realize that boy could've been me, my sister … even you?

LIEUTENANT PORTUONDO. Look, it was hard enough … Do you think it was easy for me to arrest him? I wanted the whole thing to go away … But what could I do?

MARIA CELIA. You could've let him go. He was just a boy.

LIEUTENANT PORTUONDO. I guess you don't understand my position.

MARIA CELIA. No, I think I do. It seems like outside of these walls I wouldn't recognize you. I don't really know who you are.

LIEUTENANT PORTUONDO. Don't say that …

MARIA CELIA. Even the other night when you spoke about changes, ideas, it was foolish talk.

LIEUTENANT PORTUONDO. Come here, Maria Celia … *(Takes hold of her arm.)*

MARIA CELIA. I think we should stop all of this.

LIEUTENANT PORTUONDO. Then what happened to the other night when you were open to me, full of arms? … When you took me to the patio and showed me that plant growing out of the wall … *(Pause.)* Tell me …

MARIA CELIA. I remember what I said. It's growing out of nothing with barely any soil, like us. *(She looks into the distance.)*

LIEUTENANT PORTUONDO. Then what did it mean?

MARIA CELIA. *(She looks at him. She doesn't know what to say. Turns away wanting this moment to disappear.)* When you came into this house, it seemed like everything became unknowable, unrecognizable, as if someone had robbed me of reason. There were no questions of where things might end up. I was only sure of one thing …

LIEUTENANT PORTUONDO. Of what? *(Maria Celia is silent.)* Look at me. I would have liked so many things. We had escaped this place, Maria Celia. We were one night ahead of the world.

MARIA CELIA. Do you really believe it's that easy?

LIEUTENANT PORTUONDO. What are you afraid of?

MARIA CELIA. I'm afraid of what locked-up places breed.

LIEUTENANT PORTUONDO. And what is that?

MARIA CELIA. I think everything has been defined for us. I'm locked up in here and you're out there, and we should keep it that way.

LIEUTENANT PORTUONDO. You're trying to run so fast from me you don't even know where you're going.

MARIA CELIA. No. I've been closed up in this house for a long time. Too long. It does something to your mind. A sort of blindness, that makes you close your eyes and see somebody else who's not there in front of you …

LIEUTENANT PORTUONDO. And who's that? Your husband. You see your husband in me.

MARIA CELIA. No. It's wrong. It's all wrong … It's a crime …

The same corruption that goes on out there, people bargaining for food, for a bar of soap … Except you've been bargaining with my life …

LIEUTENANT PORTUONDO. We're beyond all that, Maria Celia.

MARIA CELIA. Something is going to happen in this country soon. I can feel it coming like a storm.

LIEUTENANT PORTUONDO. What? The ringing of the bells, people dancing in the streets, celebrating nothing. Is that what you expect? Did you see the line of cars in front of the gasoline station?! Did you see how it extends for blocks? That's what's happening here. That's what people are talking about. The dregs the Russians left behind. The whole mess … Look I don't want to talk about this …

MARIA CELIA. It's what I'm holding on to.

LIEUTENANT PORTUONDO. *(Enraged.)* You know I'm tired of hearing about the fuckin' Russians! Who cares what happened in Russia! Who the fuck cares, goddamn it!

MARIA CELIA. I think you should leave, Lieutenant.

LIEUTENANT PORTUONDO. Oh, no … I'm staying right here. I'm not going anywhere. I'm not going anywhere. *(He paces back and forth.)* It's strange this thing you have over me. The worst of it is you can't make it stop, and I can't do anything about it. I've always been a clean revolutionary — as clean as can be. Not one stain on my record. You came into my life and you got inside me like a war. I don't even recognize myself. I can't even think straight anymore. You know very well I've been throwing my life away because of you, and I have far more to lose than you do.

MARIA CELIA. Do you really think this can go anywhere?

LIEUTENANT PORTUONDO. Why not?

MARIA CELIA. Yes the two of us like outlaws, criminals of some kind … There's another side to me … Something you don't want to face … I carry a whole past behind me … A whole past …

LIEUTENANT PORTUONDO. You're talking as if I didn't —

MARIA CELIA. No! You can never put yourself in my place! I made certain decisions long ago, which have locked me up in here.

LIEUTENANT PORTUONDO. Look, I've been talking to the high officials … I've been trying to get you out.

MARIA CELIA. I don't want any help. If I'm not out of this house anytime soon, I'm going on a hunger strike.

LIEUTENANT PORTUONDO. A hunger strike? And what are you going to get out of it? *(Sofia enters.)* Have you considered well what's happening out there? I suppose you don't realize what's going on. As we speak, brigades are being formed everywhere on the island, to crack down any rebellion or demonstrations ...

MARIA CELIA. That's not going to stop me. I want to change like the rest of the world.

LIEUTENANT PORTUONDO. You try to do your silly strike and the two of you will go back to point zero.

MARIA CELIA. We are at point zero, Lieutenant.

LIEUTENANT PORTUONDO. I warn you. You try and do anything, and you'll have a mob storming into this house to force-feed you ... And not with food but with every one of your books.

MARIA CELIA. You don't frighten me, Lieutenant. You use the power that's been given to you foolishly. You persecute people like me ... You pry ... You investigate my life, because you don't know what to do with yourself ... You don't know what to do with your own existence which amounts to nothing!

SOFIA. You should leave, Lieutenant. Please, just go ... just go.

LIEUTENANT PORTUONDO. Ask your sister if she has anything else to say. *(Silence.)* You want change? Then things will change! *(The Lieutenant looks at her a moment, then makes his way out of the room. He slams the door behind him. Sofia turns to her sister. Maria Celia crosses to the piano. Lights fade to black.)*

Epilogue

TWINING OUR LIVES

*The piano has been taken away. The house looks very empty.
Sofia sits on a chair where the piano used to be. She looks into
the distance. Maria Celia twines yarn as she recites a letter to
her husband.*

MARIA CELIA. "It is late at night now and I strain my eyes to see
your face. This morning I opened the door of the wardrobe and
hugged your black suit which hangs next to my clothes. Here nothing has changed, my love. If anything, the regime has reduced the
distribution of food once again. As for clothing supplies each person can expect a dress or a pair of pants every two years. Sofie hasn't
been doing well. Yesterday the only joy and little amusement we
had, was taken away from us. A group of men came to our house to
take Sofie's piano away." *(Sofia walks to the wall. She presses her ear
against the concrete partition.)* "We've started a little protest on our
roof and a hunger strike, for the time being we wait. This year the
guava tree in our patio has given so much fruit, we don't know what
to do with all the guavas. And since Sofia and I are not eating, and
the neighbors won't accept anything from us, we bring the fruit into
the house and put them everywhere, because the fragrance of the
guava reminds us of Grandma Carucha and Mami. It's like an invisible woman with a sweet perfume is staying with us, and the house
feels less empty." *(Sofia looks as if she has lost her mind.)*
SOFIA. Maria Celia, I think he's home. Come here. I thought I
heard him. Do you hear anything?
MARIA CELIA. I don't hear a thing.
SOFIA. Shshh … Come close to the wall. You hear his footsteps?
He's come back. *(Maria Celia goes along with what her sister is hear-
ing, as a way of consoling her.)*
MARIA CELIA. Yes. I can hear him.
SOFIA. You think he's alone?
MARIA CELIA. No.

SOFIA. Did you hear other footsteps? He's standing still.

MARIA CELIA. I think he's drinking.

SOFIA. Already.

MARIA CELIA. He must drink to forget. The pangs of love, Sofie.

SOFIA. Maria Celia, I used to play that song on the piano. You remember? He's playing that song in his house. What should I do Maria Celia? What should I do?

MARIA CELIA. Just listen, Sofie. Be still and listen. *(Soft piano music is heard through the wall. The music plays louder. Lieutenant Portuondo knocks on the door.)* Just listen to the music … Just listen … *(The music swells. The sisters let themselves be taken by the music, disregarding the knocking at the door. The music continues to swell, drowning out the persistent knocking.)*

End of Play

PROPERTY LIST

3 flashlights (MILITIA GUARD, LIEUTENANT
    PORTUONDO, VICTOR MANUEL)
File (MILITIA GUARD, LIEUTENANT PORTUONDO)
Baby grand piano (SOFIA)
Sofa (MILITIA GUARD)
Small oak table (MILITIA GUARD)
Radio (MILITIA GUARD, LIEUTENANT PORTUONDO)
Brass lamp (MILITIA GUARD)
Rocking chair (MILITIA GUARD)
Portrait of a lady with a fan (MILITIA GUARD)
Letters (MARIA CELIA, LIEUTENANT PORTUONDO)
Paper (MARIA CELIA)
Pin (MARIA CELIA)
Knapsack (LIEUTENANT PORTUONDO)
Two packets of letters tied with black ribbon (LIEUTENANT
    PORTUONDO)
Razor blades (LIEUTENANT PORTUONDO)
Sample package of moisturizing lotion (LIEUTENANT
    PORTUONDO)
Coffee tray with three cups of coffee (SOFIA)
Knitting needles and knitting (SOFIA, MARIA CELIA)
Permit (VICTOR MANUEL)
Handkerchief (VICTOR MANUEL)
Bag with piano-tuning tools (VICTOR MANUEL)
Shoebox with men's shoes (SOFIA)
Identity card (VICTOR MANUEL)
Package of books (LIEUTENANT PORTUONDO)
Paper bag with food (LIEUTENANT PORTUONDO)
Comb (MARIA CELIA)
Lipstick and compact (SOFIA)
Dust cloth (MARIA CELIA)
Record player and record (MARIA CELIA)
Rum (LIEUTENANT PORTUONDO)
3 glasses (MARIA CELIA)
Betel palm trees in terra-cotta containers (SOFIA)
Plant (MARIA CELIA)
Palm tree (MARIA CELIA)
Bromeliad (MARIA CELIA)
3 dry jasmine flowers (LIEUTENANT PORTUONDO)

Bundle of men's clothes (SOFIA)
Shirt (LIEUTENANT PORTUONDO)
Yarn (MARIA CELIA)

SOUND EFFECTS

Piano music
Metal prison door closing
Furniture turning over, glass breaking, objects falling
Knock at door
Rain
Cuban dance music
Drums and celebration in the distance
Voices outside and firecrackers
Swell of drum music
Sounds of the night

NEW PLAYS

★ **INTIMATE APPAREL by Lynn Nottage.** The moving and lyrical story of a turn-of-the-century black seamstress whose gifted hands and sewing machine are the tools she uses to fashion her dreams from the whole cloth of her life's experiences. "…Nottage's play has a delicacy and eloquence that seem absolutely right for the time she is depicting…" *–NY Daily News*. "…thoughtful, affecting…The play offers poignant commentary on an era when the cut and color of one's dress—and of course, skin—determined whom one could and could not marry, sleep with, even talk to in public." *–Variety*. [2M, 4W] ISBN: 0-8222-2009-1

★ **BROOKLYN BOY by Donald Margulies.** A witty and insightful look at what happens to a writer when his novel hits the bestseller list. "The characters are beautifully drawn, the dialogue sparkles…" *–nytheatre.com*. "Few playwrights have the mastery to smartly investigate so much through a laugh-out-loud comedy that combines the vintage subject matter of successful writer-returning-to-ethnic-roots with the familiar mid-life crisis." *–Show Business Weekly*. [4M, 3W] ISBN: 0-8222-2074-1

★ **CROWNS by Regina Taylor.** Hats become a springboard for an exploration of black history and identity in this celebratory musical play. "Taylor pulls off a Hat Trick: She scores thrice, turning CROWNS into an artful amalgamation of oral history, fashion show, and musical theater…" *–TheatreMania.com*. "…wholly theatrical…Ms. Taylor has created a show that seems to arise out of spontaneous combustion, as if a bevy of department-store customers simultaneously decided to stage a revival meeting in the changing room." *–NY Times*. [1M, 6W (2 musicians)] ISBN: 0-8222-1963-8

★ **EXITS AND ENTRANCES by Athol Fugard.** The story of a relationship between a young playwright on the threshold of his career and an aging actor who has reached the end of his. "[Fugard] can say more with a single line than most playwrights convey in an entire script…Paraphrasing the title, it's safe to say this drama, making its memorable entrance into our consciousness, is unlikely to exit as long as a theater exists for exceptional work." *–Variety*. "A thought-provoking, elegant and engrossing new play…" *–Hollywood Reporter*. [2M] ISBN: 0-8222-2041-5

★ **BUG by Tracy Letts.** A thriller featuring a pair of star-crossed lovers in an Oklahoma City motel facing a bug invasion, paranoia, conspiracy theories and twisted psychological motives. "…obscenely exciting…top-flight craftsmanship. Buckle up and brace yourself…" *–NY Times*. "…[a] thoroughly outrageous and thoroughly entertaining play…the possibility of enemies, real and imagined, to squash has never been more theatrical." *–A.P.* [3M, 2W] ISBN: 0-8222-2016-4

★ **THOM PAIN (BASED ON NOTHING) by Will Eno.** An ordinary man muses on childhood, yearning, disappointment and loss, as he draws the audience into his last-ditch plea for empathy and enlightenment. "It's one of those treasured nights in the theater—treasured nights anywhere, for that matter—that can leave you both breathless with exhilaration and…in a puddle of tears." *–NY Times*. "Eno's words…are familiar, but proffered in a way that is constantly contradictory to our expectations. Beckett is certainly among his literary ancestors." *–nytheatre.com*. [1M] ISBN: 0-8222-2076-8

★ **THE LONG CHRISTMAS RIDE HOME by Paula Vogel.** Past, present and future collide on a snowy Christmas Eve for a troubled family of five. "…[a] lovely and hauntingly original family drama…a work that breathes so much life into the theater." *–Time Out*. "…[a] delicate visual feast…" *–NY Times*. "…brutal and lovely…the overall effect is magical." *–NY Newsday*. [3M, 3W] ISBN: 0-8222-2003-2

DRAMATISTS PLAY SERVICE, INC.
440 Park Avenue South, New York, NY 10016 212-683-8960 Fax 212-213-1539
postmaster@dramatists.com   www.dramatists.com